The Road Guide

SLEEPING BEAR DUNES
NATIONAL LAKESHORE

Dune Grass sketch by Louise Bass

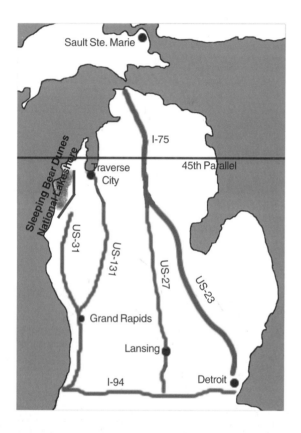

Finding the Dune Country

Sleeping Bear Dunes National Lakeshore is located in the Northwest corner of Michigan's Lower Peninsula. Major highways are indicated above for your orientation; however consult a detailed map for specific directions. Mileage from major metropolitan areas are:

From Detroit - 285 miles; From Chicago - 314 miles;
From Sault Ste. Marie - 188 miles; From Traverse City - 24 miles.

The Philip A. Hart Visitors Center and National Lakeshore Headquarters is located at the intersection of M-22 and M-72. Traverse City's Airport , Cherry Capitol Airport, connects with daily flights to Chicago and Detroit. Bus transportation is available from Traverse City.

The Road Guide

SLEEPING BEAR DUNES
NATIONAL LAKESHORE

by

Susan Stites

South Manitou Light and Keepers Station

THE ROAD GUIDE
SLEEPING BEAR DUNES
NATIONAL LAKESHORE

Published by:
Arbutus Press
2364 Pinehurst Trail
Traverse City, Michigan 49686

ISBN   0-9665316-0-4
Second Edition

CONTENTS

Introduction

Who can resist the call of the dunes? A tour of this National Lakeshore will take you to a historic lighthouse, through hardwood forests, around marshes, over rivers and to the tops of 450-foot dunes. You can spend quiet times on walking trails or cool off in small or great lakes. Hike, sail, swim, walk, ski, bike, picnic, canoe, camp, skip stones, or visit museums. The activities are endless. Or maybe what you're looking for is no activity except another layer of suntan oil and a quick trip to Z-land before dinner. There are places where you will be undisturbed. For hikers, that quiet spot on top of Pyramid Point speaks through the elements of a geologic time before ours. You can hear it again on Empire Bluff and on Pierce Stocking Scenic Drive as you view the Sleeping Bear and her Cubs, the Manitou Islands. You'll get a sense of nature by watching the sand hills give up their edges to the wind, or perhaps feel the sand, carried by gusts off Lake Michigan, stinging on your skin.

Nature is here. Peering from the cliff of a dune out onto the horizon, the only obstruction to your view is the earth's curve. Let the motion of each wave lull you to join the rhythm of this Great Lake, these Great Dunes, and this moment in time. Crystal River gently flows from a small inland lake to the Great Lake. You can canoe this crystal clear river and catch the glimmer of salmon in the fall, shore your canoe for Morel mushroom hunting in the spring, or exchange dipping your paddles for a dip in the river to cool your heels from the summer heat. As you listen to the waves and sand, the river and wind, let the calmness of nature gently relax your body and relieve your mind of daily worries. They are miles away too.

This is the home of legends. The Sleeping Bear rests here overlooking her Cubs, The Manitou Islands. The Lost Daughter of Leelanau appears on misty mornings, gliding on the water. The Ghost Fleet of the Manitou Passage lies motionless on the sandy Lake Michigan bottom. The legends live on through your photos and your memories. Let the lingering whisper of The Sleeping Bear call your sensitivity to nature awake, and when you leave, call you back to her again.

Sights of Sleeping Bear Dunes

Canoeing on the Platte River

View from Empire Beach

Fishtown in the Village of Leland

Shipwreck off South Manitou Island

Life-Saving Station at Sleeping Bear Point

Photo by Christopher F. Powell

Ferry to North Manitou Island

Sleeping Bear Dunes National Lakeshore Overview

Since the first written description of the glimmering white sand dunes by the voyageurs and Jesuit missionaries in the 1700's to Michigan's own astronaut, Jack Lousma's comment that "Sleeping Bear really stands out from space", this region remains remarkable. In 1961, U.S. Senator Phillip Hart of Michigan introduced legislation to include Sleeping Bear Dunes into the National Park System. Stewart Udall, Secretary of the Interior, assisted Senator Hart and nine years later, in 1970, Sleeping Bear Dunes became a National Lakeshore, joining Michigan's Upper Peninsula Pictured Rocks region as two outstanding natural formations deserving preservation in the National Park System.

The 72,000 acres of the Lakeshore include 35 miles of coastline on Lake Michigan, two islands, three former Coast Guard Life-Saving stations including a lighthouse built in 1871, several inland lakes, old farms houses and other historical buildings, rivers and the distinctive sand dunes. Ancient dunes, still the most dramatic feature at Sleeping Bear Bluff, Pyramid Point, Empire Bluff and on The Manitou Islands stand majestically, forever.

The Philip A. Hart Visitor Center at the intersection of M-22 and M-72 monitors the pulse of the dunes. An award winning slide show, bursting with vivid images, stirs the excitement of your anticipated stops.

Park Rangers and knowledgable volunteers will field all your questions including "Where can I see the Sleeping Bears?" The answer is there are no real sleeping bears, only legendary ones. Try to schedule your day or evening to include a Ranger guided hike or campfire talk at Platte River Point Campgrounds.

All directions and mileage outlined in this book orient from the Visitors Center.

On the Water or in the Woods

Rent a canoe, kayak or intertube for the 2-1/2 hour float down the Crystal River.

True North General Store (231-334-3090) located about .25 miles north of Glen Arbor rents floatables 7 days a week and also sells canoeing necessities like snacks, beverages and even a deli sandwich.

Crystal River Outfitters (231-334-7490) specializes in renting kayaks and also offers a fishing guide service. They are located just on the north edge of Glen Arbor.

Rent anything that floats for the easy 3 hour glide down the Platte River. This river passes through Otter Lake, where you might have to use your paddles, before rejoining the river currents.

Riverside Canoe (231-325-5622 seasonal business) located 10 miles south of Empire at Lake Michigan Road. They have a huge selection of Sleeping Bear trinkets and anything you want for canoe snacks.

Pick your season and get on the paths, water, frozen lakes or deep woods.

The Sportsman Shop (231-3343-3872) located in Glen Arbor on Manitou Ave. is open all year and rents snowshoes, Ice shanties, row boats and offers charter fishing. All the accouterments for the outdoorsperson are available as well.

Bear Bikes (231-326-6100) Rents mountain bikes for adults and children at two locations: in Glen Arbor at TNT Video on Manitou Ave. next to The Sportsman Shop and in Empire near the Visitors Center on M-22 just north of the blinking light. Rentals are available for groups if you'll call ahead. Bringing your own bike? Repair service is available too.

Sleeping Bear Dunes National Lakeshore Operations:

Location: Michigan
The Northwest corner of the Lower Peninsula

Where to Write:
Sleeping Bear Dunes National Lakeshore
9922 Front Street
Empire, Michigan 49630

Telephone:
(231) 326-5134 Main Office and TTD
(231) 326-5382 (FAX)

Internet Web site:
http://nps.gov/slbe

Camping Reservations
(800) 365-CAMP or http://reservations.nps.gov

Visitors Center Hours
Open seven days a week
Summer hours   9:00 A.M. – 5:00 P.M.
Off season 9:00 A.M. – 4:00 P.M. (closed on Federal Holidays)

Pierce Stocking Scenic Drive:
Open May–October
Winter - X-Country Skiing on unplowed drive

Maritime Museum
Open from Memorial Day through Labor Day
The grounds are always open

Fees:

Park Entrance: Park pass $7.00 (passenger vehicles, valid up to 7 days)
Annual pass $15.00 (valid thru Dec. 31)
Golden Age (62 and over, lifetime) $10.00
Golden Access (disabled, lifetime) Free
Golden Eagle (one full year, nationwide) $50.00
School groups - fees waived by prior arrangement
Commercial Tours - please inquire
Camping fees:$ 10.00 - $14.00 per night
Backcountry Camping $5.00 per night (permit required)

All person Accessible:

A wheelchair may be borrowed at the Visitor Center for use within the Park. A cassette player and audio tape tour of the handicap accessible Duneside Trail can also be borrowed for use on this asphalt covered path located near the Dune Climb. The 6 foot wide trail accommodate wheelchairs. Accessible restrooms, parking, camping and boat launches are available at designated locations throughout the park. Ask for a flyer at the Visitor Center outlining these locations.

The Manitou Islands Ferry
Located at the Fishtown docks in Leland
Manitou Island Transit
PO Box 591
Leland, MI 49654
231-256-9061

The Legend of Sleeping Bear

As told by Kenny Pheasant

"I am a descendent of the Odawa Tribe of the Algonquin Nation. And this story has been passed down from generation to generation by word of mouth by our elders. When I first heard this story of Kchi Makwa and her cubs it was told by my grandfather. And as we would gather by the fire it would rekindle all the old legends and old stories.

*L*ong long ago, in a time before the coming of the white man in his ships and sails there was a land of great woods with the tallest of pine trees. This land was near a giant and powerful lake. The land and water had no names then and now we know them as Wisconsin and Lake Michigan. In the woods and along the waters lived many birds, animals, insects and fish. Among them was a bear the Odawa people called Kchi Makwa. One spring Kchi Makwa gave birth to two cubs. The cubs played, found food and grew strong in the woods. When they were thirsty they would drink from the great lake. But this was a summer like Kchi Makwa had never seen before. The sun seemed closer to the earth, no clouds were in the sky. Each day was hot. Hotter than the one before and soon the forest became dry. Then one night, powerful winds came, then thunder, and lightening from the sky. And the lightening struck the dry forest. And immediately a terrible fire began. By morning, Kchi Makwa had gathered her cubs and took them to the great lake as the fires chased her. But once in the water they felt safe. The land was on fire and the wise mother knew her Forest was no more. Fires would remain for many days and there would be no food for her cubs. But She knew of a land across the great waters, much like this with forest and food for all the animals. Kchi Makwa did not know how far away the land was but she knew they must go.

So together they swam for two days and nights. The cubs grew weary but still they saw no land. Kchi Mokwa urged her cubs to follow but they fell behind. And on the third night another storm struck and the waves stood tall. Kchi Makwa was separated from her cubs. She too was very tired as she searched for her cubs. Finally, she moved on hoping that she would find them on the shores of the Great Lake.

It was the fourth day when Kchi Makwa finally saw the sands in the forest on the land ahead. But her cubs were not with her; she was sad. Kchi Makwa dragged herself onto the sands of the beach and shook the water from her fur. She was so weary, she wanted to sleep yet she searched the shore for her lost cubs. When she could not find them she rested, always watching the vast waters but she would not, could not eat. She waited for many days. Her cubs did not come but still she remained. Finally one day as the faithful mother waited, the Great Spirit, Manido, who is wise and created all things, took pity on her. The Manido joined Kchi Makwa and her lost cubs in the spirit world and again the mother and her cubs were happy. The spirit, Manido, was so moved by the love and faithfulness he saw, that he raise the two cubs out of the deep waters and made them islands which he named after himself. In honor of Kchi Makwa who waited so patiently, he covered the place where she lay with mounds of sand so that forever all peoples and animals would know the greatness of the sleeping bear.

These islands, sands and waters are homes to people of many cultures, home to insects, the animals, the birds and the fish. Life in the earth, on the earth, in the air and in the water. And all those who know the story of Kchi Makwa and her cubs know that life is blessed because of her faithfulness and her love."

Legend of Sleeping Bear as seen on the Original Motion Picture, "Sleeping Bear"
a film by Richard Brauer. Courtesy of Sleeping Bear Films, Inc. and Brauer Productions

Dunes Region Geology

Glaciers, made of fallen snow, compressed into a large, thickened mass of ice eons ago. Without seasonal melting, the continuous cold allowed snow to remain and build up over thousands of years. Mile high glaciers, covering this region about 12,000 years ago supplied the forces for land transformation. They scoured and gouged out the topography we see today. The glaciers crept slowly over the land, moving through existing valleys and riverbeds, shoving the land into hills and ridges, occasionally dropping large lake size chunks of ice to form kettle holes, the seed beds for today's inland lakes.

The most obvious feature of the glaciers at work is the sand, tiny bits of ground rock, a millimeter small, made of granite, feldspar, and even bits of gold. Southwest winds move the sand granules to the shoreline and beyond, covering the large lakeside hills or even a forested swale only to smother the surfaces and continue its trek until finding hindrance to its flight in any object, even the smallest blade of dune grass.

The Ghost Forests

A Ghost of a Forest, with bleached bone limbs, is all that remains of the once living Cottonwood trees. They stood vitally green leafed with smooth bark on the sandy dune until the sand-laden wind dropped their load on them bit by bit. The sand accumulated at the tree base growing higher and higher, finally covering the sky-bound tree tops. With no light or air, the trees suffocated and died entombed in their shroud of sand. With no resistance, the sand moves on; blown in the wind that brought it, releasing the branches and the tree trunks revealing the Cottonwood ghosts.

Wildlife

Sleeping Bear Dunes National Lakeshore offers a variety of habitat for wildlife. Beaver and muskrat primarily populate the wetland and inland lakes while deer, fox, raccoon, squirrels and porcupine live in the forested areas.

Most hiking paths within the Lakeshore show the evidence of White-tailed deer. Deer tracks are abundant in the Cedar swamps around Otter and Bass Lakes and on the Old Indian Trail. The best opportunities for glimpses of the deer are the in-betweens, at dawn and early morning or at dusk when the deer will graze on the west side of a dune to bathe in the last warm sun rays of the day. There are no deer on South Manitou Island but North Manitou Island has a very successful herd, so successful that the population must be "managed". Since the Island excludes natural predators, special Deer Hunts take place in October and November each year. Not only North Manitou Island targets the deer for hunting but the Park mainland does as well, excluding the heavily used areas of Pierce Stocking Scenic Drive and the Campgrounds.

White-tailed Deer

The Piping Plover

The plight of the plover contrasts with its diminutive size. This 7 inch tall, sand colored shorebird nests on level beaches, digging shallow nests for the four little eggs laid in April and May. The National Lakeshore estimates only about 20 nesting pairs remain from their once strong population of 800 pairs nesting in the Great Lakes region. They live within the park at Platte River Point, North Manitou Island and outside the park boundaries on diminishing remote shoreside locations in Michigan.

What happened to these birds? Prior to the 1900 ban on hunting, these little birds made dinner for the settlers and their plumage adorned ladies hats. But the population continued to drop, prompting a vigilant focus on habitat preservation. Not only are they included on the list of Endangered Species, locally the plovers have attracted volunteer nannies. The nannies, volunteers and Park Rangers, watch every move the birds make, especially during nesting season. These bird sitters set up their equipment at Platte River Point. Unlike the plover, the nannies with their tripods and binoculars can be easily recognized and swoop into action if you tread too close to their flock, scooting you away from the bird's nesting territory, and herding you back from the protective fences. The nannies also play an educational roll, explaining the plight of the plover to anyone who will listen, and offer glimpses of the plover chicks through their binoculars or spotting scopes.

The demise of this species parallels similar dramatic stories in the cycle of nature. North Manitou Island Rangers reported the loss of an adult female with four eggs in her nest to a hungry snowy owl. Another nanny reports that eggs from a nest in another location became dinner for a raccoon. Between animals raiding the nests and the increased recreational use of the beach, the Piping Plover is in trouble. The successful camouflage of the plover compounds its dilemma. Nearly invisible little chicks dart to and from the water's edge for food and water, but when their path is blocked by people or pets, the chicks dehydrate or starve. The Endangered Species Act of 1986 makes it illegal to harass or harm these shorebirds.

Adult Piping Plovers have a black crest on their forehead and a black neck ring. The most distinguishing markings are their bright yellow-orange legs.

Tracking the Birds

The Official Park Information Journal, "View from the Dunes" is free of charge at the Visitors Center. The following is an excerpt from the publication.

"This fall and winter some of these piping plovers were seen wintering in Texas, Florida and Georgia. One of the chicks from the Platte River nest was seen on Marco Island, Florida. The male from one of the Platte River nests was seen at South Padre Island, Texas. The female from this same nest was seen on St. Simons Island, Georgia. (Separate vacations?)

A male piping plover that nested in Vermillion Pt. in Michigan's Upper Peninsula was also seen this winter on Marco Island. This bird was a chick hatched on North Manitou Island."

Black Bears in Sleeping Bear

Rangers report an occasional visitor requesting to see the live Sleeping Bears but the only bear they'll see are those of legend. The native black bear population is primarily found in the Michigan's Upper Peninsula but on occasion, bears are spotted in the park, although their visits are infrequent. The black bear roams for hundreds of miles, searching for food, shelter and a mate. Generally, they are not dangerous but they can be aggressive when protecting their cubs. They are in continuous search for food in the summer months. Overturned logs and rotted tree stumps in pieces are signs that the bear is searching for insect larvae, ants, acorns, berries or the honey from a bee hive.

The Legend of Sleeping Bear represents just one of the many Native American stories symbolizing the respect for bear, often portrayed with formidable and sometimes supernatural powers. In many cultures, the bear was looked upon with such reverence that members of the culture were not allowed to speak the word for "bear". Instead, they referred to the animal with varied euphemisms such as "big feet" or "black beast".

Black Bear

Wildflowers

Show-time starts even before the snow melts with Dutchman's Breeches poking their eager faces toward the warm spring sun. They look like upside down pantaloons dangling on arched stalks about 5 inches tall. Platte Plains and Indian Trail both harbor these early bloomers that cover the forest floor. Hepatica's delicate little flowers sprout up from the liver shaped leaves of this beauty. Find this member of the buttercup family in the dryer woods of Empire Bluffs Trail, Platte Plains and Indian Trail's "Green arrow trail".

A favorite show stopper, the Trillium, a protected wildflower due to its scarcity, won't seem scarce along Shauger Hill Rd. or along the Pierce Stocking Scenic Drive. Floral blankets of white to pink delicate tri-leaved flower are worth waiting out the winter months just for the visual treat in May. The bloom lasts for two weeks, starting out white and fading to pink in the last few days of bloom. New flowers rise from seed clusters falling on the soil but take two years to germinate, and another few years to bloom.

Bloodroot, usually one of the first spring wild flowers, shows up in April, in the Beech-Maple Forests of Empire Bluffs and again on Shauger Hill Road. The delicate white flower, perched on a blood red stalk, lasts only two days.

Not all the wildflowers in the Lakeshore are indigenous species or desirable. Baby's Breath, a florist's staple, often dried and brought indoors for eye-catching displays of tiny white flowers, grows on these dunes, crowding out native plants. Recently, volunteers, under the guidance of the National Park Service, began "weeding-out" these undesirables making space for the dune flowers: Bearberry, Beach pea, and the threatened Pitcher's Thistle among others growing in the dunes region. Another alien wildflower, the Purple Loosestrife, a spiked magenta-flowered wetland invader, can cover acres of wetlands crowding out native aquatic plants valuable to waterfowl and other wildlife.

Shipwrecks

In the last century, the legendary Great Lakes storms grasped more than 50 victims in its turbulent seas and unpredictable squalls and sent them heads-up and bottoms-down to the depths of this inland passage. Now held for all time in the 282 square mile Manitou Passage Underwater Preserve, they are on display in this outdoor muscum. From the lumber toting steamers of the late 1800's to the modern freighter of the 1960's, the Ghost Fleet of Sleeping Bear is a collection of vessels spanning 100 years. The most popular wreck, The Francisco Morazan, lies only partially submerged, close to the Southwest shore of South Manitou Island. It crashed on a shoal in 1960 during a December snowstorm and now rests almost on top of a wooden steamer, The Walter L. Frost, that met its fate in 1905.

Fate took another turn in 1911 when a steam barge, The Three Brothers, sailing out of Boyne City, Michigan sank close to shore. This wreck was never found despite many attempts of wreck finders in the 1970's and 1980's until April, 1996, when two employees from the Lakeshore noticed that a sand bar, long noted as a part of the Islands shoreline, vanished over the winter and in its place lay the Three Brothers, nearly intact as the day she sunk in 1911. The 160 foot vessel lies just 150 feet from the south end of the island in 15 feet of water. The fascinating story of the ship's last passage to Manitou is detailed in the Nov/Dec 1996 issue of Michigan History Magazine.

The Manitou Passage Underwater Preserve attracts thousands of scuba divers each season. It offers good visibility, shallow depths, and a variety of artifacts that speckle the sandy bottom. Along with shipwrecks in the preserve, the old dock pilings still stand with their tips at water level in Glen Haven, Port Oneida, Aral, and both North and South Manitou Islands.

Shipwrecks and other underwater cultural resources, such as prehistoric sites, piers, wharves and other structures, are valuable and nonrenewable. More than just shipwrecks, these resources are irreplaceable records of our cultural history.

"Take nothing but pictures, leave nothing but bubbles".

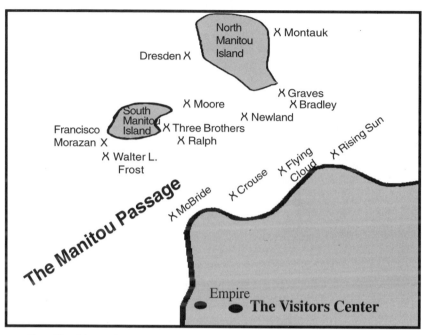

Over fifty shipwrecks belong to the Ghost Fleet of Sleeping Bear now part of the
Manitou Passage Underwater Preserve

The wreck of the Liberian freighter Francisco Morazan, partially submerged on the
Southwestern shores of South Manitou Island

The Southern Route

Empire Bluff Overlook and Hiking Trail

Platte Plains Trail/Otter Creek

Otter Lake and Bass Lake

Platte Plains River and Platte River Point

Platte River Campground

Old Indian Hiking Trail

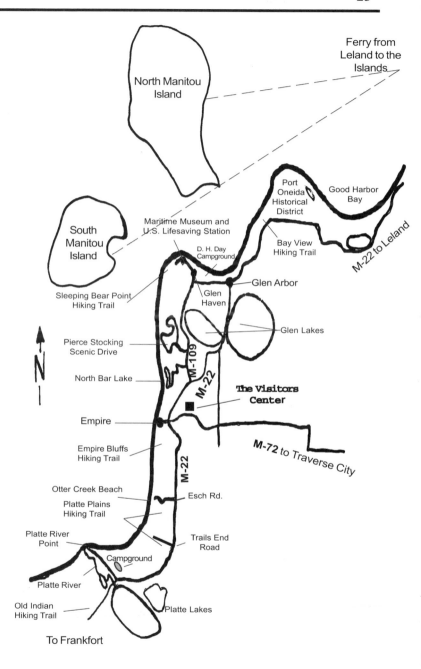

North Manitou Island

Ferry from Leland to the Islands

South Manitou Island

Port Oneida Historical District

Good Harbor Bay

Maritime Museum and U.S. Lifesaving Station

Bay View Hiking Trail

M-22 to Leland

D. H. Day Campground

Glen Arbor

Sleeping Bear Point Hiking Trail

Glen Haven

Glen Lakes

Pierce Stocking Scenic Drive

M-109

N

M-22

North Bar Lake

The Visitors Center

Empire

M-72 to Traverse City

Empire Bluffs Hiking Trail

M-22

Otter Creek Beach

Esch Rd.

Platte Plains Hiking Trail

Platte River Point

Trails End Road

Campground

Platte River

Old Indian Hiking Trail

Platte Lakes

To Frankfort

Empire Bluff Overlook and Hiking Trail

Empire Bluff Overlook Directions: From the intersection of M-22 and M-72 near the Visitor Center, turn left onto M-22 traveling 1.5 miles to Wilco Road. Turn right onto Wilco Rd. The parking lot is about .5 miles on your left.

A top-of-the-world view marks the end of the 350 foot Empire Bluffs Hiking Trail. Watching the Chicago to Mackinac Island sailing race or a 1,000 foot freighter passing through the Manitou Passage is like watching little toy boats, floating on a vast pond. To the north, views of Empire Beach, South Bar Lake, Sleeping Bear Bluffs (including The Sleeping Bear Dune which appears as a small hill on top of a sand dune) and South Manitou Island, while Platte Bay is visible to the south. The trail is mildly vigorous with a discernible incline. Old farm orchards, fallow fields and a beech-maple forest are attractions on the way to this overlook.

Empire Bluff's view includes evidence of the slow continuous assault from the shifting sand, covering once living trees, leaving a "Ghost Forest".

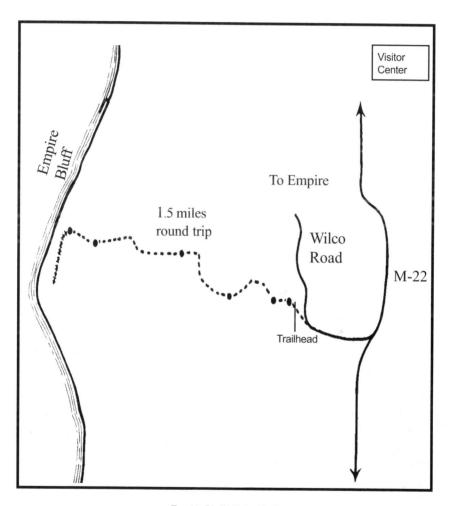

Empire Bluff Hiking Trail

Platte Plains Hiking Trail / Otter Creek

Platte Plains Hiking Trailhead and Otter Creek Directions: From M-22 take a right turn on Esch Road, 3.9 miles from the Visitor Center and 1.2 miles from Wilco Road. The beach and trailhead are at the end of Esch Road. An alternative route is Norconk Rd., a seasonal road closed in the winter.

One of the favorite beaches for locals is Otter Creek Beach. The spring-fed Otter Lake about 4 miles south feeds the Creek. Otter Lake, Bass Lake and Deer Lake are connected but deadfall and shallow channels make only Otter Lake accessible for canoeing. Access to Otter Lake is from Trails End Road. Miles of lakeshore with adjacent warmer creek waters present a nice swimming option to the chillier Lake Michigan where the temperature is often too cold to swim. Another option is to hike the beach north to Empire Bluff.

There is a historic region here also, the ghost town of Aral. Originally called Otter Creek or "the Krik", the name changed to Aral (for the European mountain region) since the U.S. Post Office already registered a village named Otter Creek in southern Michigan. Settled slowly in the late 1800's, 150 men and their families lived in this isolated community whose livelihood was primarily logging and sawmill operation. The remnants of an old loading dock may be evident if the water level is low enough.

Access to the Platte Plains Hiking Trail is located here. Three loops totaling 14.7 miles can be used for skiing or hiking. Otter Creek loop's 4.6 miles is mostly flat terrain. Bass Lake Loop, 3.5 miles, provides access to Bass Lake and Deer Lake. Lasso loop, 6.6 miles, is challenging, with sections of steep hills and views of Lake Michigan. Most trails follow the crest of ancient shoreline formed through glacial lake stages. The White Pine backcountry campground requires a back country permit.

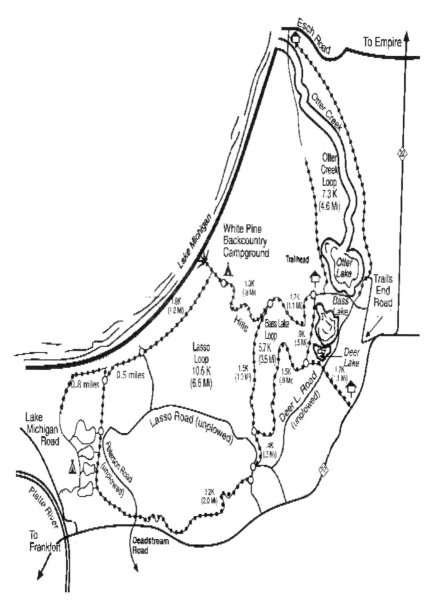

Platte Plains Trail System

Otter Lake and Bass Lake

Otter Lake Directions: From M-22, turn right onto Trails End Road, 6.1 miles from the Visitor Center, bear left at the fork and then stay straight. The boat launch is on the right side of the road. Bass Lake is at the end of the road.

Access to Otter and Bass Lakes is located here. There's a dock for small frys to fish and a boat launch just down the road as you come in. At this little-used site, you'll find the quiet retreat for which Northern Michigan Lakes are noted. A trailhead for the Platte Plains Hiking Trail System is clearly marked.

Some large trees are located on Trails End Road. A Red Pine 6.7 feet in circumference is located on a foot trail. From the intersection of M-22 and Trails End Road, drive .3 miles to the fork and bear right. Go another .3 miles and park on the right at the steel gate. The foot trail exits the woods at the right. Walk approximately .25 miles along the trail. The Red Pine is on the right, at the edge of a large clearing, surrounded by Birch and Tamarack. If you reach the wooden footbridge you have gone too far. Another big tree is a Jack Pine. Return to the fork, turn right, and drive down Trail's End Road. At .2 miles turn left onto Deer Lake Road, which is unsigned. Go another .2 miles and the tree is on the left, easily visible from the road. Its circumference is 5.2 feet. Finally, a Balsam Fir, 4.3 feet in circumference, is located at the end of Trails End Road. Park in the parking lot and take Platte Plains Trail to the north. The tree is on the right side of the trail, by Otter Lake.

Left: Branchlet from a Balsam fir. Characteristic fragrance and tradition makes this a favorite Christmas tree

Right: A cone from a Red Pine Tree. Average trunk size of Red Pine is 2 to 3 feet in circumference.

Platte River and Platte River Point

Platte River Directions: From M-22 heading south, turn right at Lake Michigan Road, 10 miles from the Visitor Center. Lake Michigan Road is just across the road from the Lake Township Hall. Once you have turned onto Lake Michigan Road, the campground is on the right, the river on the left. There are several picnic grounds along the river. The swimming beach is 2.5 miles away, at the end of road.

Canoeing and tubing are the favorite activities on this section of river. Canoes, tubes and lots of Duney memorabilia are at the Riverside Canoe Livery just over the bridge on M-22. The current is slow enough that the whole family will enjoy the float. The famous Platte River flows from Platte Lake, about 2 miles east of M-22 through Loon Lake until it flows into Lake Michigan. Known as the first river in Michigan to release the coveted game fish, Coho Salmon, the river is replete with spawning salmon in the fall. Although a fish weir set up downstream harvests most of the spawning species, fishermen speckle the shores from September through early November. The State of Michigan Platte River Fish Hatchery is located just up the river. It is the largest hatchery of its type east of the Mississippi.

Canoeing the Platte River delivers a delightful surprise at the end of a gentle ride. The river carries sediment which settles out at its mouth, forming a sand spit. Another surprise, this is a nesting area for the endangered little bird, the Piping Plover. Watch where you step! Their camouflage is so perfect, they're almost invisible. Some areas are off limits during nesting.

The combination of river and lake make great swimming options. The warmer river water may make swimming more comfortable when the chilly water temperatures of Lake Michigan are less appealing.

Good views of Empire Bluff and Sleeping Bear Bluff from the shoreline as you look to the north. To the south, you can see Point Betsie, the site of another historical lighthouse and former Life-Saving Station. Picnic grounds, restrooms and plenty of parking make this a very popular and sometimes crowded recreation area.

Platte River Campground

Platte River Campground Directions: From M-22, turn right onto Lake Michigan Road, 10 miles from the Visitor Center. The campground is .3 miles on your right.

179 sites in total. Reserve a camp site by calling 1-800-365-CAMP (2267) or stop in. In addition to regular RV and tent camping sites, there are walk-in sites (150 foot walk) that are away from the traffic and crowds allowing more space to spread out and enjoy the quiet nature sounds around you. Groups of 7 persons or more can reserve space at the group camping site. Camping fees are $14.00 per night with an additional charge for electrical hookup and park pass. Ask about the "Exploring with a Ranger" program usually scheduled every day in the summer and also the evening Campfire Programs nightly next to the Ranger's Station. These programs enrich the experience of visiting the Dunes.

The campground is built on a former Indian Camp. Prior to construction of the Platte River Campground, an archeological site was located and excavated. Artifacts found: a large quantity of rocks used for campfires, small flint chips used for making tools, pottery, some arrowheads and two pieces of copper. These items were dated between 250 A.D to 1250 A.D., fitting the Woodland Period of Native American Cultural History. The site remains a campground for today's campers as it has for nearly two thousand years.

Archeological dig at this campground found a large quantity of rocks split from the heat of campfires, small flint chips used in toolmaking, pieces of pottery and a few arrowheads. Charcoal from prehistoric campfires dated between 244 A.D. and 1253 A.D.

Old Indian Trail

Old Indian Trail Directions: From M-22 heading south, the trailhead is 13.7 miles from the Visitor Center, on your right. Watch for the sign for Old Indian Trail.

"Old Indian Trail" is what you might expect from its name, old Indian trails that lead from established camps to and from the shores of Lake Michigan. Two, 2-1/2 mile loops wind through varied landscapes. The Black Arrow trail leads up and down the dunes and around cedar swamps giving you the feeling of being enveloped in dunes. This is the most scenic of the two loops and provides a challenge to cross country skiers in the winter. The Green Arrow trail follows more level ground. On both loops, deer tracks are everywhere. The swampy areas and dense forest provide a haven for mosquitoes. Best to douse yourself with extra strength insect repellant for a most enjoyable hike. The short leg of both loops turns out through a "ghost forest" and over to Lake Michigan and a beach only hikers can access.

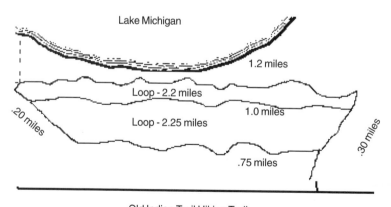

Old Indian Trail Hiking Trail

The Northern Route

North Bar Lake
Shauger Hill Hiking Trail
Pierce Stocking Scenic Drive
Windy Moraine Hiking Trail
Dune Climb, Duneside Trail
Glen Lake Beach
Glen Haven Historic Village
U.S. Life-Saving Station/Maritime Museum
Dunes Hiking Trail
D.H. Day Campground
Alligator Hill
Pyramid Point Hiking Trail
Bay View Hiking Trail
Port Oneida Historical District

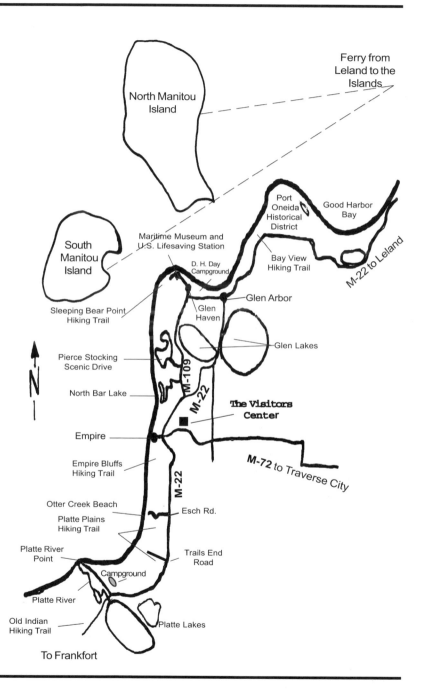

North Bar Lake

North Bar Lake Directions: From the Visitor Center, turn right onto M-22, 1.7 miles to Voice Road. Turn left onto Voice Rd. then turn right on Bar Lake Rd.   North Bar Lake is 1.2 miles at the road marked "Seasonal Road". There is a paved parking area with vault toilets. A short walk leads to the south side of North Bar Lake.

One of the precious tucked away gems of Sleeping Bear is North Bar Lake, a calm warm pond that issues into Lake Michigan via a short channel ideal for wading and floating toy boats. Big water/little water, and one or the other always in the lee because of the low dune between. Lugging the picnic gear is a little cumbersome because of the sandy commute to the beach.   Lake Michigan, just over the hill, sometimes connects. Fragile dunes and fragile plants have made this area a Nature Preserve. The federal list of rare and endangered species includes plants and animals found in this region. The Pitcher's Thistle, Monkey's Flower, Broomrape and the Prairie Warbler are found here. North Bar Lake is one of the few remaining lakes with an outlet to Lake Michigan. However storm waves often close the outlet with a sand blockade alternating, in time, with higher water that opens the channel. Signs funnel foot traffic onto a boardwalk over the low dune to reduce human impact and promote dune preservation and restoration.

Pitcher's Thistle is on the Federal list of endangered species. It is found only on dunes of Lakes Michigan, Huron and Superior.

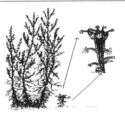

Broomrape is associated with the tall wormwood. It has no chlorophyll and derives nourishment from the roots of the Wormwood.

Shauger Hill

From M-22 turn left onto M-109 which is 2.2 miles from the Visitor Center. Proceed on M-109 and follow the signs to Pierce Stocking Scenic Drive. The scenic drive is on your left. A Park pass is required and can be purchased at the entrance. Shauger Hill trailhead is just to the right of the Kiosk.

Shauger Hill can be a leisurely walk in the woods in summer or a very challenging cross country ski run in winter due to the extreme uphill and downhill sections. For skiers, this trail ties in to the longer Pierce Stocking Scenic Drive. For a backroad tour, drive along Shauger Hill Rd. The forest floor is bursting with Trillium and hidden morel mushrooms in the spring.

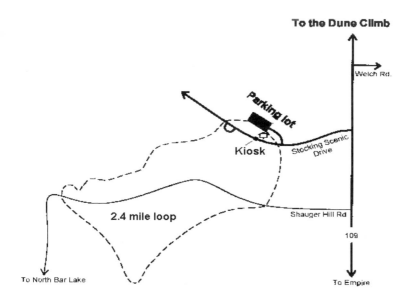

Shauger Hill

Pierce Stocking Scenic Drive

Pierce Stocking Scenic Drive Directions: From M-22 turn left onto M-109 which is 2.2 miles from the Visitor Center. Proceed on M-109 and follow the signs to Pierce Stocking Scenic Drive. The scenic drive is on your left. A Park pass is required and can be purchased at the entrance.

A 7 mile paved drive for bikes or cars with numbered stops interpreted through a pamphlet available at the kiosk. Two hiking trails lie within the scenic drive, Cottonwood Trail and Shauger Hill. The Cottonwood Trail's 1.4 mile loop explores the rolling dunes, dune grasses, shrubs and wildflowers. The loose sand can make this short walk a workout and the summer's sun intensifies the heat at ground level. Take water and wear shoes. Shauger Hill is described on the previous page.

Stop #1 is the wooden covered bridge, and beyond it at stop #2, a spectacular view of the Glen Lakes. If there is only time for one stop, walk out to the Lake Michigan Overlook. You'll get the closest look at the lady herself, The Sleeping Bear, a mere shadow of her former self due to wind erosion. It's worth the walk onto a boardwalk, but secure your hat. The wind on the Lake Michigan sometimes blasts stinging, blowing sand. But on days when the wind is calm, the views are unforgettable.

Picnic Mountain is the ideal location for a lingering lunch, perched on a knoll with 180 degree view of paradise that photos will never capture like your senses will. North Bar Lake Overlook, another picnic spot toward the end of the drive, may be an option and is always less crowded.

Bikes are permitted on this drive. Try renting bikes back at Empire and park your car or campers in the designated parking area just beyond the kiosk.

Pierce Stocking Scenic Drive winds through the forests to the lakeshore and back again, leaving you with the idea that something phenomenal took place here. From the dramatic actors, the sand dunes, to the bit players like sandreed grass, they all join in the famous production of "The Dunes Show", playing any time you want to see it.

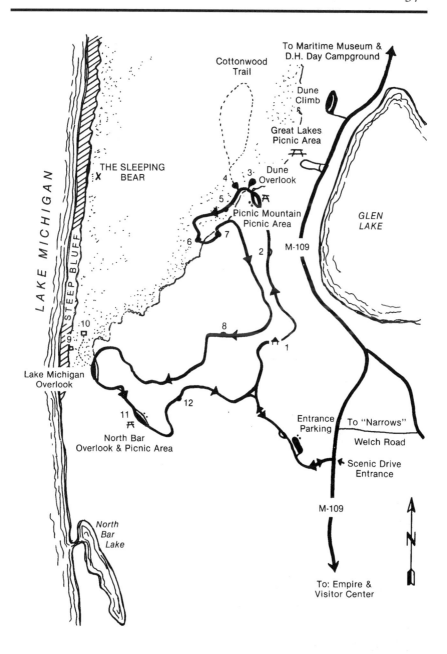

Pierce Stocking Scenic Drive

Windy Moraine Nature Trail

Windy Moraine Nature Trail Directions: This hiking trail is .1 miles from the entrance to Stocking Scenic Drive. Look for Welch Road on the right as you are heading North. The parking area is visible from M-22.

Trail maps, available near the trailhead, describe the features of this nature hike using self-guiding numbered posts along the way. This 1.5 mile hilly trail is a good way to introduce biodiversity and ecology to children's vocabulary. A wayside exhibit along the trail explains aspects of soil and teases us with the question, "Did you know that Michigan has an official state soil?"

Most of the trails in Sleeping Bear Dunes offer a view and Windy Moraine is no exception with overlooks of Glen Lake and sweeping views of the valley below.

In the winter, Cross Country Skiers find this trail a nice "warm-up" before tackling some of the other longer ski trails in the Park.

Windy Moraine Nature Trail

The Dune Climb and Duneside Trail

The Dune Climb Directions: Take a left turn from Pierce Stocking Scenic Drive onto M-109 heading north. The Dune Climb is 2 miles ahead on your left. You can't miss it. A large parking area, gift shop, and accessible vault toilets are at this site.

For generations, families head up this sand mountain, reach the top of its 300 feet and run back down to do it all over again. A sneak preview of what's over the dune: more sand, and a 1-1/2 mile trek to Lake Michigan. If you're planning a day at the beach armed with coolers and beach chairs, this is not the best route to take. The sand is hot and the trail is long. But do climb as many times as your calf muscles will allow. Amble over to the base of the dune's north side to examine a measuring post lying flat on the ground. It determines the movement of the whole sand dune. On average, the dune moves inland at 3.5 feet per year.

The 1.8 mile paved Duneside trail, located on the north side of the parking lot, is accessible for all visitors, including mobility or visually impaired. Borrow the interpretative audio tape produced for this trail from the Visitor Center. There are accessible restrooms near the parking lot.

The Dune Climb

Glen Lake Beach

Glen Lake Beach Directions: Turn left onto M-109 heading north from the Dune Climb and watch for Glen Lake Beach on your right. The beach is 6 miles from the Visitor Center.

After a romp on the Dune Climb dip into Little Glen Lake. The public beach is outfitted with plenty of benches, picnic tables and grills. The water temperature is always warmer than Lake Michigan but cool enough to be refreshing.

Regional history never escapes the history buff. The D.H. Day sawmill operated in this location in the late 1800's The mill processed timber from the surrounding forests, often floating hundreds of logs to the mill site. Processed lumber made its way the three miles to the dock at Glen Haven by rail. From there, the ships carried it various parts of the country including Chicago following the Great Chicago Fire of 1871.

Glen Haven Historic Village

Glen Haven Historic Village Directions: Follow M-109 heading north. Glen Haven is 7.1 miles from the Visitor Center. There are signs pointing the way to Glen Haven and the Maritime Museum..

Originally named Sleeping Bearville, this village started as a wooding station, owned by C. C. McCartey for fueling steamships sailing the Manitou Passage between Chicago and Buffalo. Sleeping Bear Inn, built by McCartey in about 1863, stands as the landmark of this sleepy ghost town. It housed the woodcutters needed to chop and haul the cordwood fuel for the steamship engines and in the 1930's served as a tourist hotel during the Dunemobile era. Dunemobile Scenic Dunes Rides, a business operated by Marion Day Warnes, D.H. Day's daughter, and her husband, Louis, really began the recreational use of the dunes but were discontinued in the late 1970's to protect the fragile dunes.

In its lumbering heyday, Glen Haven was a typical company town whose lumberjacks and dock workers received coupons as paychecks to be redeemed for food and supplies at the company store.

The red barn on the east side of the road served as a blacksmith shop, shoeing horses and repairing equipment. Other buildings served the local workers as shops and additional housing for the married woodcutters and their families. Great strides are underway to preserve these historical buildings and open them to visitors. Funds for restoration projects come from user fees.

The Cannery, on the shore of Lake Michigan now houses boats for restoration and display. It really was a canning plant for local crops, cherries in the summer and apples and cider in the fall, from nearby orchards. The canned fruit was shipped out on steamers, providing industrial diversity to the region facing the decline of the lumber business in the early 1900's. David H. Day, one of the leading influences on the community's development, built the Cannery.

The Sleeping Bear Inn by the shores of Lake Michigan in Glen Haven provided housing for the woodcutters in the 1860's. Later, the Inn operated as a tourist lodge.

The Cannery, built by D.H. Day, processed local fruit which was loaded onto waiting ships at the dock just yards away. Later, trucks shipped the products as roads improved. With improved roads, the dock was no longer used for any area industry.

D.H. Day

Hired as a manager for the Northern Transportation Company in 1878, 24 year old Day managed the sawmill operation near Glen Lake, the docking and wooding operation at Glen Haven and a 1,600 acre farm. By 1880, the wood supply was nearly exhausted. To maintain the area industry , he raised a second growth forest and obtained acres of land to the north and south to carry on a sustained logging operation and farming.

Cut from the same cloth as many ambitious entrepreneurs of the time, Day worked obsessively to acquire wealth through agriculture, land deals and development. One such plan was to rescue the company town of Sleeping Bearville (Glen Haven) by buying the town's land at rock bottom price from the failing Northern Transportation Company he worked for as a young man. He platted the land into streets and lots. The lots were never sold and the town withered with its supporting industry. Undaunted, he continued his personal campaign to develop the region as a tourist playground by selling his second growth forest, Alligator Hill just south of Glen Arbor, to American Park Builders of Chicago in 1922. Day Forest Estates was a "resort deluxe" plan with polo fields, tennis courts, golf courses, a landing strip, marinas and (rumor circulated) plans to build a summer White House for President Calvin Coolidge. Constructing roads through the forest and building pillared entrances to welcome the wealthy estate owners wanting to live in social exclusivity, Day's future looked prosperous, but he died in 1928 and all construction stopped when the depression hit in 1929. The same expectant roads of D. H. Day Forest Estates are the Alligator Hill hiking paths and ski trails today.

On M-22 just north of Pierce Stocking Scenic Drive stands the regional landmark, the D.H. Day Farm. It is privately owned today.

Former property of the National Transportation Company, the D. H. Day Farm was a showplace named "Oswagotchie". By 1903, the 400-acre farm was described as one of the best appointed in the country.

Maritime Museum and Lifesaving Station

Maritime Museum Directions: Follow M-109 heading north. The Maritime Museum is 7.6 miles from the Visitor Center on M-209. There are signs pointing the way near the intersection of M-109 and M-209.

The Great Lakes fresh water seas transported thousands of vessels as commerce increased following the Civil War. Sailing vessels and steamers used the channel between the Manitou Islands and the mainland, the Manitou Passage, while traveling between Chicago and the Straits of Mackinac. The Manitou Passage allowed access to a natural harbor on South Manitou Island, the only natural harbor between the Island and Chicago from frequent and violent storms that brewed in the Great Lakes. The passage also saved sailing time, about 60 miles, but at the cost of treacherous currents and shoals.

During the severe winter of 1870, 214 sailors lost their lives in shipwrecks on the Great Lakes with only shoreside residents to attempt rescues. The alarming number prompted Congress to appropriate money for the U.S. Life-Saving Service and the construction of Life Saving stations along the coast of the Great Lakes began. By 1900, there were sixty stations erected including one on North Manitou Island, Sleeping Bear Point and South Manitou Island. In the brief life of the U.S. Life-Saving Service, 1871 to 1914, over 170,388 people were rescued with an astounding success rate of 99%.

The crew for the Life-Saving Service were recruited from the local residents whose main qualification was the ability to row an open boat in a storm. Surprisingly, there was no requirement for surfmen to be able to swim. Since the crew was part of the community, often the villagers would watch the daily practice sessions. These scheduled routines were the same for every station throughout the Service. Monday, drill and practice with the beach apparatus; Tuesday, boat practice; Wednesday, signal practice; Thursday, beach apparatus drill; Friday, practice restoring the apparently drowned; Saturday, housekeeping and grounds maintenance. The weekly surfboat practice provided great entertainment for the locals who watched the drills, including the crowd pleasing capsized surfboat practice.

Beginning as a semi-volunteer effort, the U.S. Life-Saving Service built its station on Sleeping Bear Point, an unstable dune, later moving to its present location. It developed full-time lighthouse keepers, often called "Captain", and crews that trained on the specialized equipment used to rescue sailors or passengers on ill-fated vessels. Near the Maritime museum, the boathouse still features the rail used to wheel the boats lakeside for rescue. Many of the ingeniously designed original devices used by the U.S. Life-Saving Service and later the U.S. Coast Guard are displayed.

The surfmen, chosen for their skill at rowing an open boat in a storm, were often men from the community. A crew of six to eight men ranked from #1, the most highly skilled through #8, usually a junior crew member. The surfmen were well respected in the community for their courage and skill in rescues. Surf boats were wheeled to the lake on rails extending from the boathouse to the lake. Other equipment was pulled by horse or harnessed men through the sand in the most dismal weather conditions. These heroes weathered poor pay, rigorous standards, and physical exhaustion to be called the "Life-Savers". (Photo Courtesy of the National Park Service)

Men from the Coast Guard gave demonstrations of the Lyle Gun in the 1920's just as Park Rangers and Park Volunteers do today. The box in the foreground held the coiled rope attached to a weight which was inserted into the barrel of the small cannon. Propelled by gun powder, the projectile sailed through the air to its target, a distressed vessel. Once the ropes were secured onto the threatened vessel, the Breeches Buoy could be used to tow the unfortunate victim to shore. (Photo Courtesy of the National Park Service)

The Beach Cart was the work horse of this ingenious rescue method, saving precious time by transporting the gear. The Breeches Buoy, dangling from its safety line, towed the victims to safety. (Photo Courtesy of the National Park Service)

Stations operated under very exacting regulations. The keeper's daily journals reported all activities and shipwreck assistance. All duties, including the most important beach patrols, were performed flawlessly, with a lesser performance a reason for dismissal.

The beach patrol was a set 2 to 4 mile shore walk in all the worst weather. Surfmen slogged through blizzards, driving rain and sleet, hurricane force winds or violent lightning storms on constant vigil for distressed ships. These men carried a beach lantern and two or three Coston signals, a brightly colored flare used to signal a distressed ship that help was on the way. Should a patrolman find a wreck, he returned to the station, reported it and returned with the crew, no matter how tired he was because there were no spare crewmen.

A constant day and night watch from the station tower brought its own dangers. During a lightning storm in 1903, the tower at Sleeping Bear Point was struck by lightning. The tower was destroyed and the surfman on watch killed.

Crewmen memorized rules and procedures for "restoring the apparently drowned". This practice paid off for one shipwreck victim on South Manitou Island. The crew worked on a child for 20 minutes before he recovered. After an hour and 20 minutes of effort on the father, they gave up when a physician pronounced him dead. Reports of life saving efforts lasting four hours with eventual success gives credence to one Captain who said," No man's ever drown until he's dead."

In 1915 the U.S. Life-Saving Service merged with the Revenue-Cutter Service, to form the U.S. Coast Guard. Approximately 2,200 men of the Life-Saving Service and 1,800 from the Revenue-Cutter Service continued the operations and organization of their old service but under the new joint name of U.S. Coast Guard.

The Maritime Museum is restored to its 1930's appearance and is open in the summer. A daily reenactment of breeches buoy rescue with Raggedy Ann & Andy as shipwreck victims delight all visitors especially children, who are encouraged to participate.

The Sleeping Bear Point Hiking Trail

The Sleeping Bear Point Hiking Trail Directions: Turn right as you exit the Maritime Museum parking area. The Trailhead is at the end of the road about .3 miles.

Landslides in 1914, 1971 and again in 1995 advise hikers to exercise caution to stay away from the edges of the dune. The sand and wind movements off Lake Michigan together with a sharply sloping Lakebed create the physics of these periodic landslides. This event was witnessed by some men from the U.S. Life-Saving Station and documented in a 1914 *Traverse City Record Eagle.*

"A queer freak of nature occurred when a portion of the extreme end of Sleeping Bear Point, a mile north of Glen Haven disappeared into Lake Michigan. The account says 'a number of life savers of the station had been attending a party in the town and had returned by the path up over the point at two clock Sunday morning and on reaching the lighthouse had looked back and had failed to see the land over which they had come. They started out to investigate and found that a large portion estimated between 15 and 20 acres had gone into the Lake."

In 1997, the same location was identified as having a large underwater landslide, leaving the area again unstable.

This trail envelopes you in desert-like atmosphere with nothing but sand for miles. The loop is a 2.8 mile hike that can be strenuous and downright grueling on hot days. Bring water, foot gear and sunscreen. Your reward for this hike is a good look at a "ghost forest" and a sand formation called the "Devil's Hole". Hike out onto the beach for a quick dip before returning to your car.

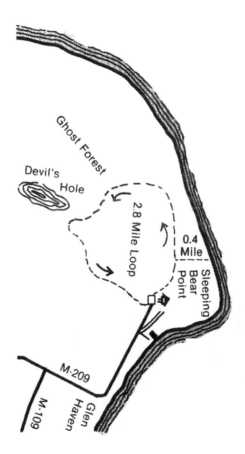

Sleeping Bear Point Hiking Trail Map

D.H. Day Campground

D. H. Day Campground   Directions: The campground is 7.4 miles north of the Visitor Center on M-109 between Glen Haven and Glen Arbor.

One of the first Michigan State Parks established in 1932 along with Mackinac Island State Park, D.H. Day offers great, woodsy camping. Log Cabin Restoration undertaken by the Friends of Sleeping Bear, a nonprofit volunteer group, gives a rustic feel to the Park Interpretation Program housed here. The 88 sites are plenty big and private with easy access to miles of Lake Michigan Beach. No showers or flush toilets. Group camping for 7 people or more must be reserved. For the rest of us it's first come, first served. The reservation number for group camping is 1-800-365-CAMP.

Built in 1925 and recently restored by the volunteer group, Friends of Sleeping Bear Dunes, Inc., this log cabin serves as an interpretive center for the D. H. Day Campground. The land, donated by D.H. Day, became the first State Park in Michigan . (Photo courtesy of The National Park Service)

Alligator Hill

Alligator Hill Directions: From D. H. Day Campground turn left onto M-109 to Stocking Road just a short .2 miles away. Turn right onto Stocking Road. The trailhead is on your left. An alternative route is from Day Forest Road off M-109 near the Dune Climb.

Beyond the entrance to the former D. H. Day Forest Estates, Alligator Hill offers great hiking and skiing. It even has a two way out and back trail for a scenic lookout. The open fields on the Advanced loop put a skier up against the wind. Prepare for the bite on windy, cold Michigan mornings. This is the only trail in the Park that allows Horseback riding! The charcoal ovens, near the trailhead, are remnants of Pierce Stocking's logging enterprise. He processed the waste wood in these ovens in the pre-brickette days of the 1950's to produce charcoal for outdoor grilling. The bagged charcoal sold locally and was shipped to other locations.

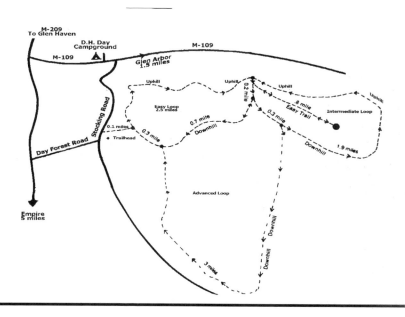

Pyramid Point Hiking Trail

Pyramid Point Trail Directions: Take M-22 heading north to Port Oneida Road. Turn left onto Port Oneida Road following its bend to Pyramid Point trailhead which is 2 miles on your left.

This mildly strenuous 1.5 mile hike climbs up to one of the highest dunes in the Park. The view is breathtaking. The Manitou Islands seem to float over the lake between the waves and the clouds giving them the mystical image of the Legend of Sleeping Bear. If you're lucky, conditions will be right for a four island view with North and South Fox visible in the northeast. While it may be tempting to run down this bluff, please refrain from doing so. Every footprint displaces the sand, leading to more erosion and eventually, a lesser dune than the majestic Pyramid Point.

Four hundred feet below, just off the shoreline, lies the *Rising Sun*, a shipwreck visible if the winds have moved the sand to reveal its weathered skeleton. The *Rising Sun* was grounded by heavy waves and winds only 200 feet from shore with 32 people on board in 1917. Some passengers swam to shore, others used the lifeboats on board but everyone landed safely. Later, one man found on the wreckage reportedly slept through the whole episode and was transported safely to the shore in the morning. This shipwreck and many others are part of the Manitou Passage Underwater Preserve. A 1911 shipwreck recently discovered is The Three Brothers just 150 feet off the south end of South Manitou Island. Like the Rising Sun, sand movement hides and reveals the lake-claimed vessel.

Part of the face of Pyramid Point plunged into the water sometime around July 3, 1998 when it was reported by a local resident. The landslide covered an estimated 225 feet of beach, while debris jutted 125 feet into the lake and piled more than 25 feet high. In February, 1995, a dune slide at Sleeping Bear Point dumped more than 35 million cubic feet of dune into the water, extending debris more than two miles offshore. Estimates are that the Pyramid Point slide is only about the quarter of the size of the Sleeping Bear Point slide. Researchers believe that the slides happen during heavy rain or snowmelt periods, when large amounts of water sink through the dune and increase fluid pressure between grains of sand. The higher pore pressure weakens the forces which hold the sand together, making large portions of the bluff weaken susceptible to slides. Caution signs remind visitors of the possibility of unstable dunes in this area.

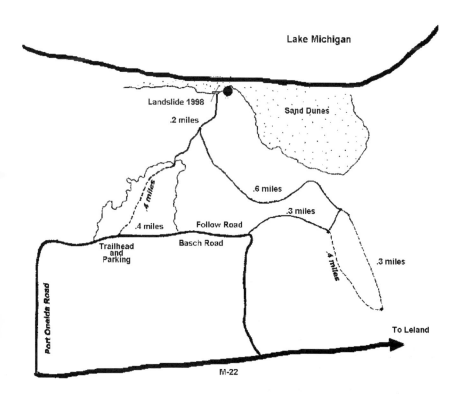

Pyramid Point Hiking Trail

Bay View Hiking Trail

Bay View Hiking Trail Directions: From M-22 heading northeast, turn left onto Thoreson Rd. 12.4 miles from the Visitor Center. The trailhead is on your left.

Hike or ski in but carry your own water. This hiking trail has a variety of hillside overlooks, historical farm sites and prairie-like fields. Hilly terrain provides a good lookout point on the loop north of Thorcson Road. This 11 mile trail, divided into shorter loops, gives you an opportunity to explore parts of Port Oneida Historical District. The north loop passes by The Miller Barn, all that is left from a sprawling 202 acre farm. The Charles Miller family met with tragedy when Mrs. Miller perished in a house fire in 1940. A grove of black locust trees used for wagon tongues and fence posts still grows by the side of the barn as does a 300 year old apple tree. The century old barn itself, an icon of an era, is supported by four large boulders for its foundation.

The Werner Family Cemetery is to the northwest of the Miller barn, on a bluff overlooking Lake Michigan and the Manitou Islands. The isolation of the cemetery and German inscribed headstones reflect the proud heritage and lonely outpost of this second family to arrive in Port Oneida.

The Burfiend/Garth Farm is at the corner of Port Oneida Road and Miller Road. This 100 year old farm house was moved here from another location closer to Lake Michigan. The farm house is privately owned.

Port Oneida School House is visible on the west side of Port Oneida Road near its intersection with M-22. Built in 1860, this school also served as a community center for the village. Notice the row of Sugar Maple trees to the south. They were planted by the students in celebration of Arbor Day and tapped in subsequent years for maple syrup.

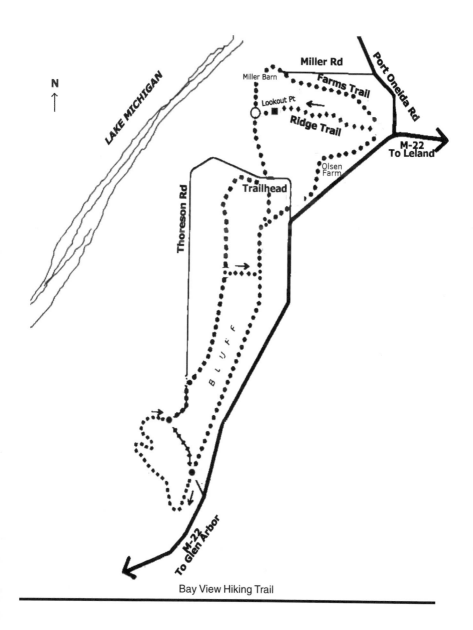

Bay View Hiking Trail

Port Oneida Rural Historic District

Port Oneida Historical District Directions: Follow M-22 to Port Oneida Road on your left, 16.4 miles from the Visitor Center. Please respect the privacy of residents in this area,

Port Oneida Historical District, recently placed on the Register of National Historic Places, includes 3,400 acres and 99 buildings. It stands with only a handful of historic landscapes in the country of its quality and size and is the only one in the Midwest in public trust. It is most like Cades Cove in the Great Smoky Mountains National Park, a historic farm community open to visitors to tour cabins, barns and outbuildings.

Port Oneida's buildings, skillfully erected by primarily German immigrants during the 1860's, display old world craftsmanship in the style that is typical architecture of the region and era. Most of the farm grounds are accessibly to the public; however, a few houses remain in private ownership. Drive by the Kelderhouse Farm, just off M-22 on Port Oneida Road. Thomas Kelderhouse and Carsten Burfiend led the community economic development by building a loading dock for ships to take on the cordwood needed as fuel. Like many villages, the lumber era meant prosperity for these communities; however the era ended with the depletion of wood and the community turned to agriculture for its livelihood. Farming on sandy soils limited their success and by 1908 all the buildings, except for the Kelderhouse residence, at the original Port Oneida townsite were abandon.

One of the most endearing qualities of Port Oneida is the island like community. The "sense of enclosure" created close-knit families frequently gathering for worship and community events. The 65 acre Kelderhouse farm was a gathering place for the Port Oneida farmers and their families. Once used as a grocery store, telephone headquarters and post office, it is still surrounded by the Maple trees Port Oneida students planted to make maple syrup in the spring each year.

Further north on Port Oneida Road is the Burfiend family farm site. The first to settle in Port Oneida, the family lived in a log cabin on the beach. However, the rough winter winds and pirate attacks prompted a move to a larger log cabin up the bank and away from the lakeshore where it is now marked by a lilac clump in the field next to the road. The lilacs also mark the burial site of several members of the Burfiend family. The farm is located on both sides of the road. Two farm houses still stand, one built by Carsten and Elizabeth Burfiend's son, Peter in 1893, from hand hewn beams, most likely from the original log cabin; and the other built in 1930, by Peter's son Howard. At that time, most of the farm buildings were moved across Port Oneida Rd. The barn and pumphouse burned in 1982.

Many descendents of Port Oneida farmers still live in the region of the National Lakeshore. "Farming at the Water's Edge" by Marla J. McEnaney et. al. is an excellent source of the cultural and agricultural history of Port Oneida. This source details building construction, summarizes family histories, and farm layouts.

The struggle to preserve the old farmsteads of Port Oneida is evolving. Like all National Parks, funding to preserve all the buildings inherited when the Lakeshore was established in 1972, falls behind the need. The transition from private to public ownership fuels the controversy of old building preservation. Why tear down buildings vacated by people living in the Park District when many have cultural and historical value? If they don't demolish the buildings, why ask people to leave their homes? A quandary, partially solved by the Historic District Preservation Plan, concentrates on developing partners with the Park Service. These Partners contract for use of an existing building with promises to restore them, from their own financial resources and network of volunteers. One such partner and the first to occupy a farm in Port Oneida is Shielding Tree Nature Center, a 7 year old non-profit organization without a home.

Shielding Tree Nature Center's mission is in harmony with the Park's: To nurture an understanding, appreciation and concern for the natural world. In the summer of 1999, this organization will use the Lawr Farm for its changing seasonal displays and as a staging area for their many events all geared toward nature education. Local biology specialists, such as an entomologist (insect specialist), bird specialist, frog specialist, or just good old biologists lead hikes or plan special events to enhance the nature experience of children and their families. They always plan a full moon walk. To inquire about the latest schedule call (231) 271-3189 or stop in at the Lawr Farm in Port Oneida. As with all non-profit organization, your donations are appreciated.

The historical and cultural landscapes and districts of the Lakeshore are scattered all across the 72,000 acre Park. Port Oneida is just one of the recreational and educational resources for the Lakeshore and community. There are other old farmsteads dotted along the landscape south of Empire, near Good Harbor Bay and on South and North Manitou Islands. Some of the buildings house seasonal park help and others for Park interpretation but most wait for preservation.

Between 1860 and 1865, at least 15 land claims document Port Oneida's beginnings as a farming community. From the smallest claim of 30 acres to the largest of 160 acres, pioneers cleared the land, built homes and barns, and began raising corn, potatoes, wheat, rye, oats and varieties of garden vegetables. Farming on these sandy soils proved to be limited but community support strong. During the late 1800's, threshing time brought neighbors together, sharing the steam powered threshing machine, supplying cordwood for its fuel, and at day's end a communal dinner prepared by the farm women.

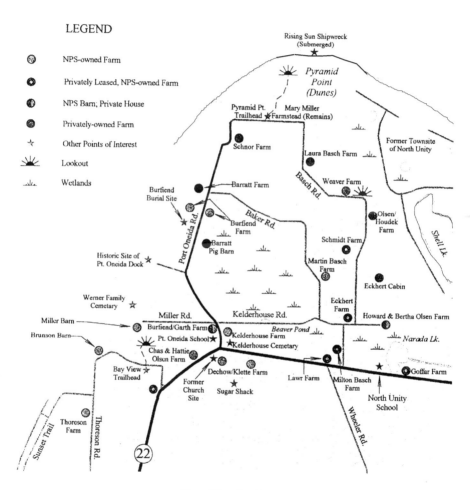

LEGEND

- 🅰 NPS-owned Farm
- ◉ Privately Leased, NPS-owned Farm
- 🅱 NPS Barn; Private House
- 🅲 Privately-owned Farm
- ⋆ Other Points of Interest
- ☀ Lookout
- 〰 Wetlands

Rising Sun Shipwreck (Submerged) ⋆

Pyramid Point (Dunes)

Pyramid Pt. Trailhead ⋆
Mary Miller Farmstead (Remains)

Former Townsite of North Unity

Schnor Farm

Laura Basch Farm

Basch Rd.

Weaver Farm

Olsen/ Houdek Farm

Shell Lk.

Barratt Farm

Burfiend Burial Site

Baker Rd.

Burfiend Farm

Schmidt Farm

Barratt Pig Barn

Historic Site of Pt. Oneida Dock

Martin Basch Farm

Eckhert Cabin

Port Oneida Rd.

Werner Family Cemetary

Miller Rd.

Kelderhouse Rd.

Eckhert Farm

Howard & Bertha Olsen Farm

Miller Barn

Burfiend/Garth Farm

Beaver Pond

Brunson Barn

Pt. Oneida School

Kelderhouse Farm

Kelderhouse Cemetery

Narada Lk.

Chas & Hattie Olsen Farm

Bay View Trailhead

Dechow/Klette Farm

Lawr Farm

Milton Basch Farm

Goffar Farm

Former Church Site

Sugar Shack

North Unity School

Thoreson Farm

Sunset Trail

Thoreson Rd.

Wheeler Rd.

㉒

Map of Port Oneida
(courtesy of the National Park Service)

North Manitou Island

The Manitou Islands are accessible by ferry operated by the Manitou Island Transit Company located in Leland. The ticket office is located in Fishtown. Manitou Island Transit, PO Box 591, Leland, MI 49654, 231-256-9061, (fax) 231-271-2601

North Manitou Island remains a wilderness area, mainly for the adventurous backpacker and camper. Travel this 32 acre island paradise by foot only and plan on staying overnight. The ferry makes the crossing only three times a week transporting passengers to the most remote part of Sleeping Bear Dunes National Lakeshore. Once on land, you'll be greeted by 20 miles of shoreline, 400 foot dunes and an inland lake, Lake Manitou. There may be warmblooded greeters as well since the Island supports a healthy herd of deer. In 1927 four male and five female deer were introduced to the island with the hope that they would multiply to a number large enough for hunting. Due to lack of predation, 2,000 deer were counted during the fall and winter in 1981 causing overbrowsing. To manage the deer herd, The National Park Service allows limited hunting on the Island in October and November with special permits.

A few buildings, old summer cottages, hunting lodges and small family cemeteries date from the logging and farming days. The U.S. Life-Saving Station, built in 1855, is the oldest building in the Park and the oldest of its type on the Great Lakes. It sits along the beach in front of "cottage row", a group of summer homes built in the 1900's. The village buildings are in disrepair but restoration is planned by the National Park Service.

To camp, a backcountry permit and fee payment must be completed before camping. The Village Campground contains eight designated campsites, two fire rings and one outhouse. Fires are permitted only in community fire rings in designated campgrounds. Water is available at the Ranger Station. .

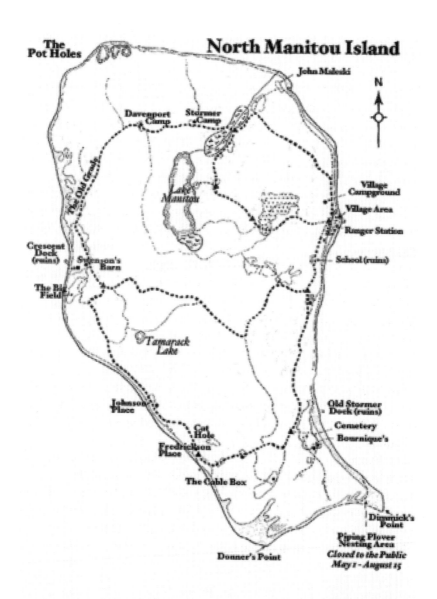

North Manitou Island

The Pot Holes

John Maleski

N

Davenport Camp

Stormer Camp

Village Campground

Village Area

Ranger Station

Lake Manitou

Crescent Dock (ruins)

Stevenson's Barn

The Old Grade

School (ruins)

The Big Field

Tamarack Lake

Johnson's Place

Old Stormer Dock (ruins)

Cemetery

Cut Hole

Bournique's

Fredrickson Place

The Cable Box

Dimmick's Point

Piping Plover Nesting Area
Closed to the Public
May 1 - August 15

Donner's Point

South Manitou Island

Located about 17 miles from the boat landing in Leland, South Manitou Island is a perfect destination on a warm sunny summer's day. Start by making reservations with the Manitou Transit Company, pack your lunch, grab your shades and most comfortable walking shoes and climb aboard. The hour and a half ferry ride starts from the dock in Leland early in the morning (check the current schedule) and returns about 4 PM. Crossing the Manitou Passage can be a memorable adventure in itself. It is an international shipping lane frequented by both 40 foot sailboats and 1,000 foot freighters. On the island, the century old 100 foot lighthouse stands out with a dramatic pose against the sky. Check the schedule for the Park Ranger led tour of the lighthouse and nearby U.S. Life-Saving Station.

The 1870 census listed 14 households and 76 people on the Island. Twelve households farmed. The isolation made for subsistence farming, selling meager, if any, surplus crops to passing ships or mainland markets. But the isolation had advantages as well, most notably the ability to raise pure strains of grains, achieved by pure pollination. Photos show prize winning crops of Rosen Rye raised on the Island in the early 1900's.

The Valley of the Giants is about a 6 mile round trip; there the Virgin White Cedars escaped the extensive logging on this island date back hundreds of years. In fact, a huge fallen cedar dated to the time of Christopher Columbus.

The wreck of the Morazan is not far from the Giant Cedars. It is partially submerged off the west shore of the island. The Liberian freighter grounded on a snowy night in November of 1960 signaling a Coast Guard helicopter and two Coast Guard vessels to rescue 15 people from the freighter.

There is a tram offering tours of the Island's midsection where the old village, schoolhouse, and cemetery are located. The tour lasts about an hour and includes the fascinating island history.

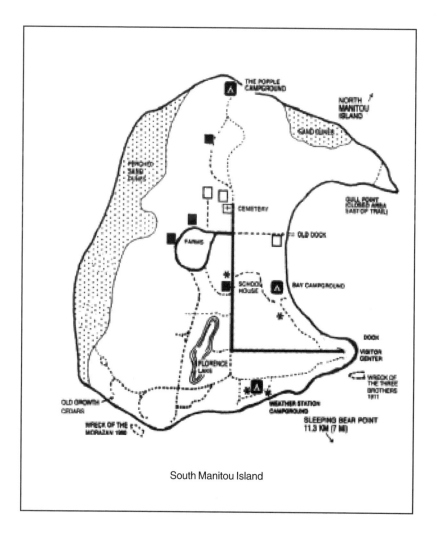

South Manitou Island

Order Form

Arbutus Press
2364 Pinehurst Trail
Traverse City, Michigan 49686

Telephone Orders: 231-946-7240

The Road Guide: Sleeping Bear Dunes National Lakeshore $7.95
A 60 page guide to Michigan's Sleeping Bear Dunes. Hiking trails, beaches, maritime museum and regional history described.

Sleeping Bear Dunes National Lakeshore Audio Tour Tape $11.95
A 60 minute audio self-guiding tape to play in your car as you drive through dunes. Starting at the Visitors Center ending at Glen Arbor. Includes stops at Pierce Stocking Scenic Drive and other popular sites in the Lakeshore.

Leelanau Peninsula Audio Tour Tape $14.95
A 60 minutes audio self-guiding tape to play in your car as you drive a 100 mile tour of Michigan's beautiful Leelanau Peninsula. Includes legends history and geology of the region.

Mackinac Island Audio Tour Tape $14.95
A 60 minute audio self-guiding tape for Mackinac Island's legends, history and natural features. Listen in your car on the way to the ferry or take your "Walkman", play the tour tape and enjoy the 8 mile road around the Island

Please send the following titles:	Qty	Price
Ship to (Shipping and handling included in price if in the U.S.):		Total